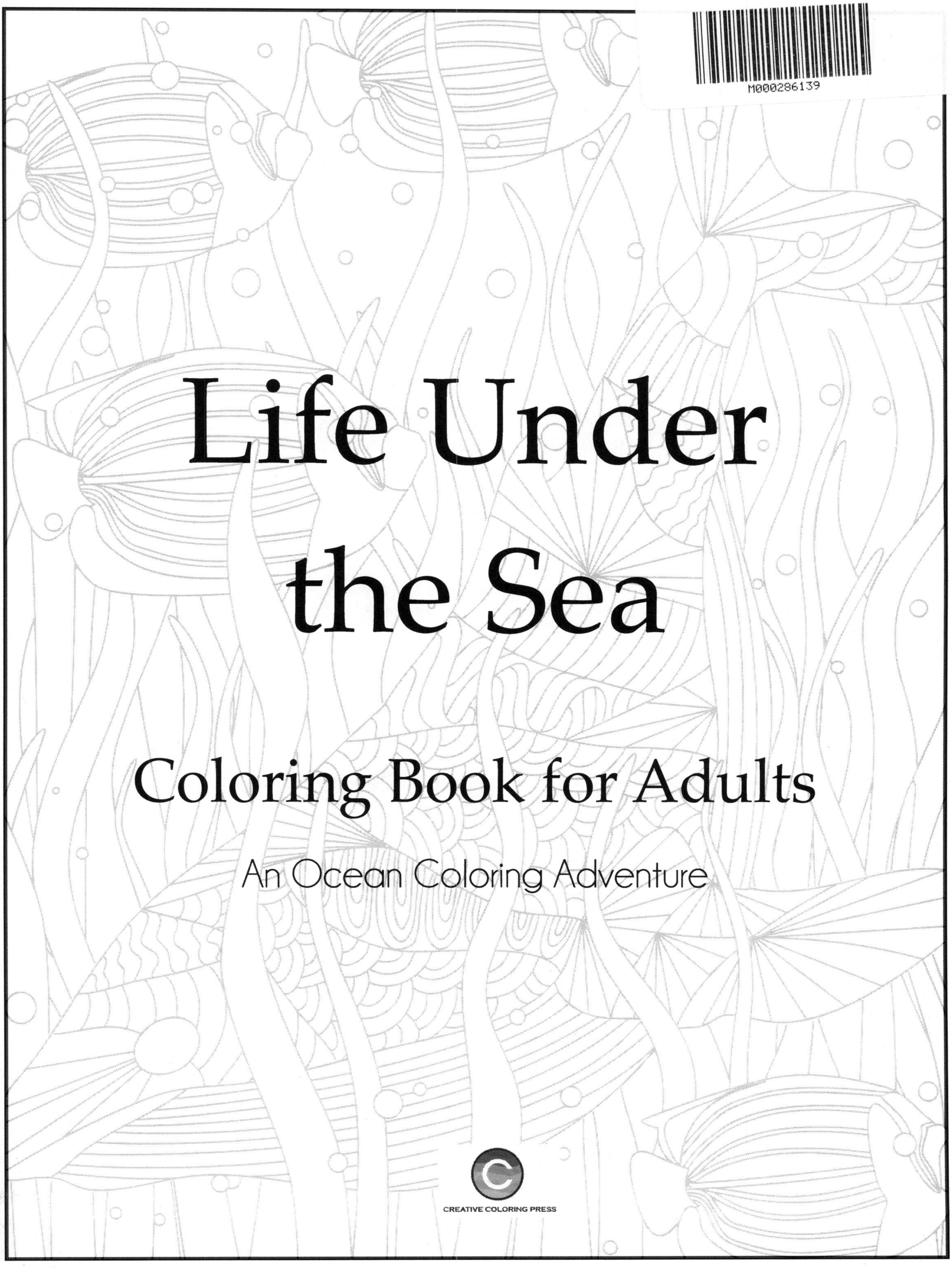

Life Under the Sea

Coloring Book for Adults

An Ocean Coloring Adventure

CREATIVE COLORING PRESS

First edition: 2017

Disclaimer/Limit of Liability
This book is for informational purposes only. The views expressed are those of the author alone, and should not be taken as expert, legal, or medical advice. The reader is responsible for his or her own actions.

Photo credits: Shutterstock

This Book

Belongs To

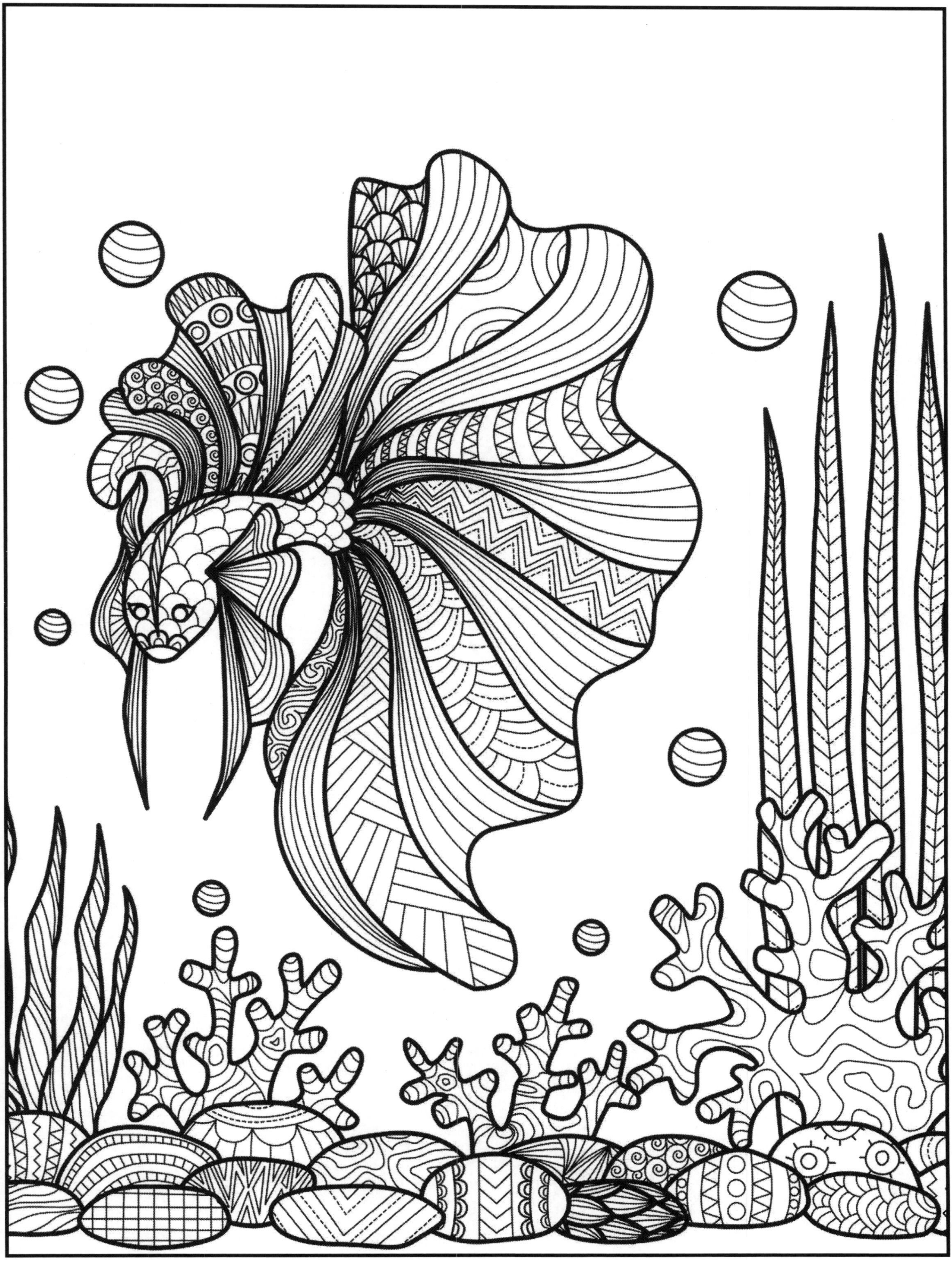

summer

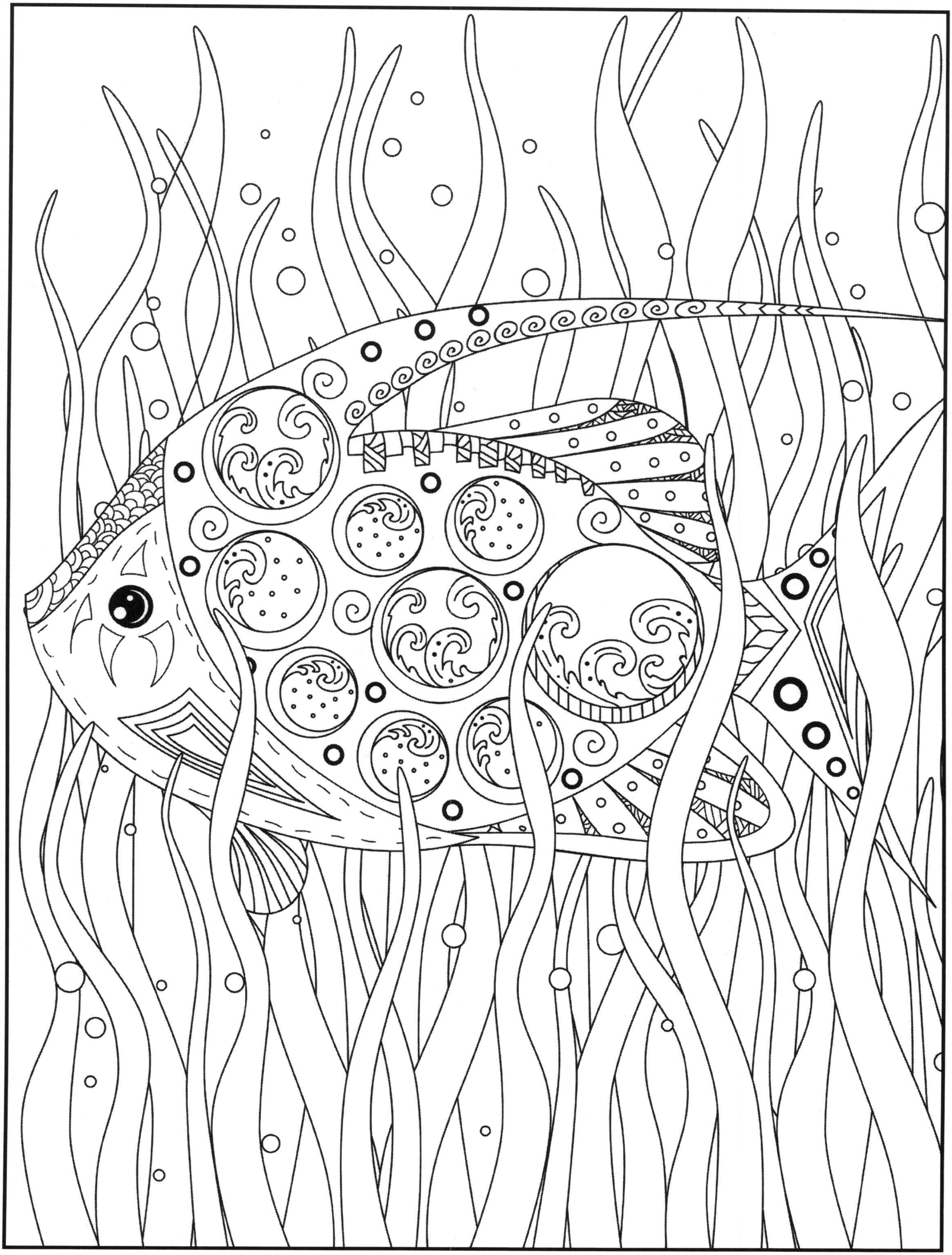

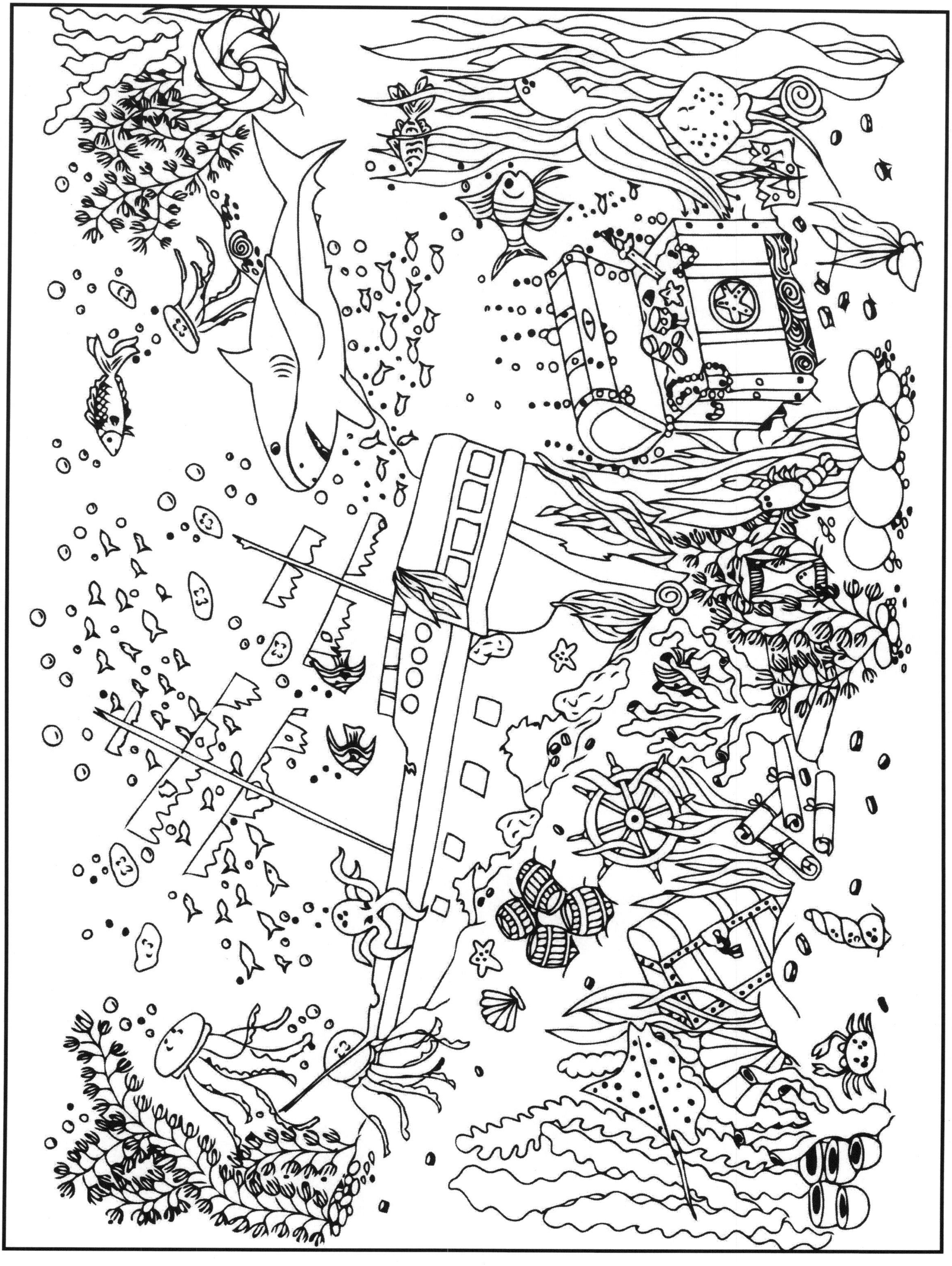

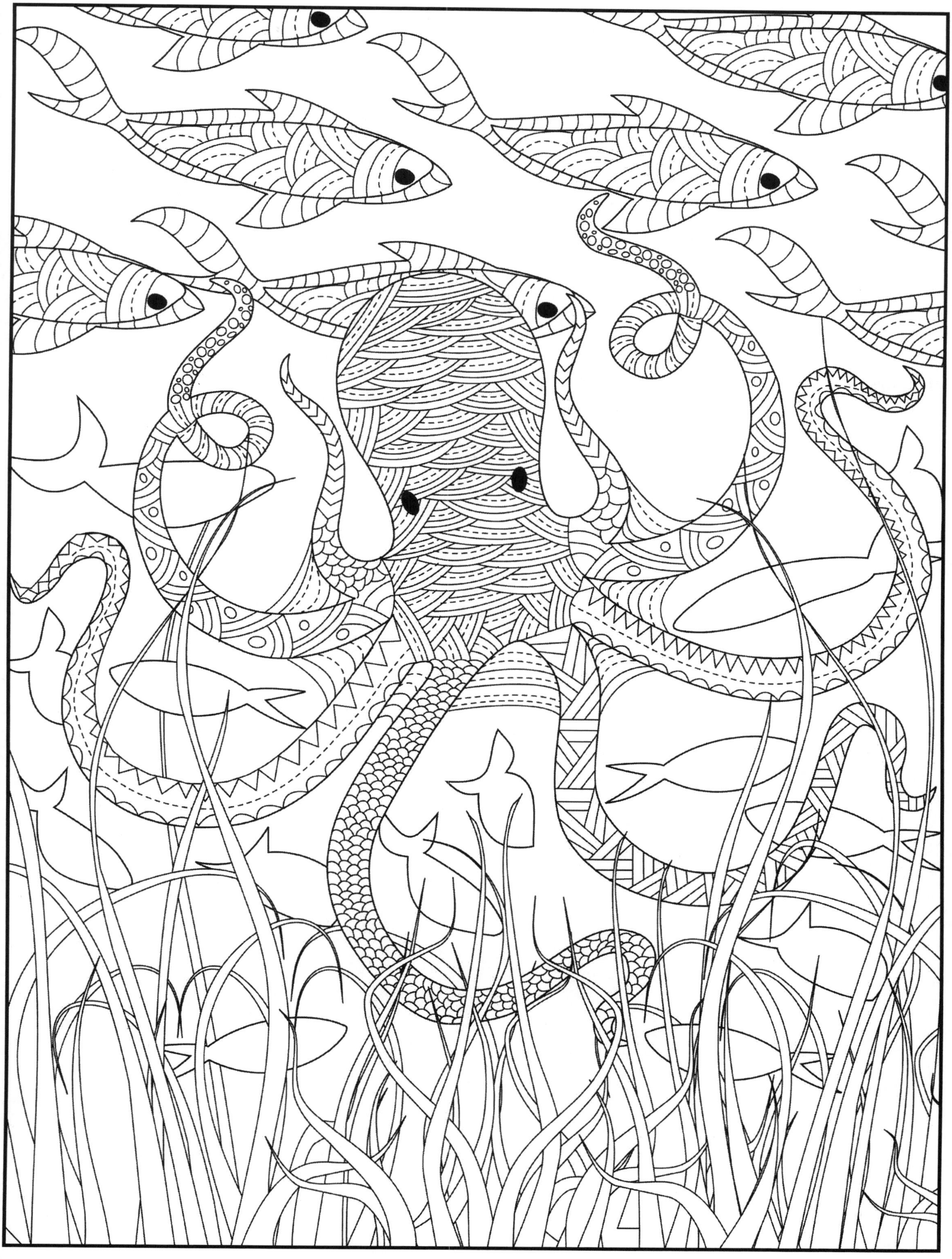